EyeOpeners!

ALL ABOUT ANIMAL VISION

Monika and Hans D. Dossenbach

CONTENTS

Published by Blackbirch Press, Inc.
260 Amity Road
Woodbridge, CT 06525

©1999 by Blackbirch Press, Inc.
First Edition

e-mail: staff@blackbirch.com
Web site: www.blackbirch.com

Printed in Hong Kong

10 9 8 7 6 5 4 3 2 1

First published in 1996 by
Kinderbuchverlag Luzern (Sauerländer AG), Aarau, Switzerland

Library of Congress Cataloging-in-Publication Data

Dossenbach, Monique.
[Augen Auf! English]
Eye Openers! / by Monika Dossenbach and Hans D. Dossenbach. — 1st ed.
p. cm.
Includes bibliographical references and index.
Summary: Introduces the many types of eyes found in the animal kingdom, including those of the dragonfly, adder, gorilla, lynx, and vulture, and tells how animals use their unique eyes to survive.
ISBN 1-56711-216-1 (alk. paper)
1. Eyes—Juvenile literature. [1. Eye. 2. Vision. 3. Animals.]
I. Dossenbach, Hans D., 1936– . II. Title.
QL949.D6713   1999   97-32130
573.8'8—dc21   CIP
                                                    AC

BLACKBIRCH PRESS, INC.

WOODBRIDGE, CONNECTICUT

EYES LIKE YOURS

Our eyes help us in many ways. We see the world in lots of colors. We can see things at great distances, such as mountains that are many miles away. Our eyes adjust so we can also see things that are very close, like a hamster that is squirming in our hands.

Gorillas are a lot like humans. A gorilla sees its surroundings in much the same way we do. Of all the animals, a gorilla's eyes are most like ours.

The eyes of a gibbon, like those of other apes, see colors well. This helps them as they roam the forest, looking for ripe fruits to eat.

Like us, monkeys can show their feelings with their eyes. This guenon monkey peers with curiosity out from the green vegetation of its surroundings.

KEEPING AN EYE OUT

Cats' eyes see straight ahead. Their eyesight is very good in dim light but cats can't see many different colors. They are excellent at judging distances in front of them. This is important, because otherwise a cat might leap right past a mouse it is hunting!

When someone sees especially well, people say he or she has "eyes like a cat." In fact, wildcats like this lynx have extremely sharp eyesight.

Rabbits and hares have eyes on the sides of their heads, which helps them to notice enemies approaching on all sides.

Hawks have eyes that magnify objects like binoculars do. These birds see about eight times better than humans, and can spot prey from high in the air.

Even though its eyes are small, a field mouse can usually see a hawk flying above. Most often, this allows the mouse time to scurry into its hole.

EYES IN THE NIGHT

Often, you can tell a lot about an animal's vision by looking at the size of its eyes. This eagle owl—with very large eyes—has excellent vision. Most owls, however, do not readily distinguish colors, despite the fact that they do have cones (color sensors) in their eyes. At least one owl—the tawny owl—can see colors.

Wildcats and other animals of the night have mirror-like eyes that pick up light and help them to see in the dark. That's why their eyes shine back when you catch them in the flashlight!

"Red-fronted lemur" is the name of this primate from Madagascar. Thanks to its large, mirror-like eyes, it can jump safely from branch to branch, even at night.

Insect-eating bats and other small bats usually have small eyes, and many see poorly. These bats rely on echolocation—sound waves—to find their way in the dark.

UNDERWATER EYES

Most frogs don't see very clearly. But they do notice every movement around them and they react very quickly. Such quick reflexes allow frogs to jump after an insect flying by, or to avoid danger by diving underwater when a hungry stork or heron appears.

Mudskippers have round eyes on the top of their heads so they can peer above the water while staying mostly covered. A mudskipper is actually a fish that can move around on land!

Living in the ocean, a seal needs eyes that work well underwater. This seal sees well beneath the ocean's surface as well as on land, if there is bright light. But on a gray day, it sees poorly.

Deep sea fish that live in darkness probably can't see colors. But fish that live near the surface of the water often use colors to recognize members of their group.

BIG-EYED BIRDS

Most birds have big eyes relative to their heads. Birds depend on their eyesight. Their hearing is often only average, and they can hardly smell at all. But they see the world clearly and in many colors. When a big-eyed ostrich holds its head high, nothing escapes its notice!

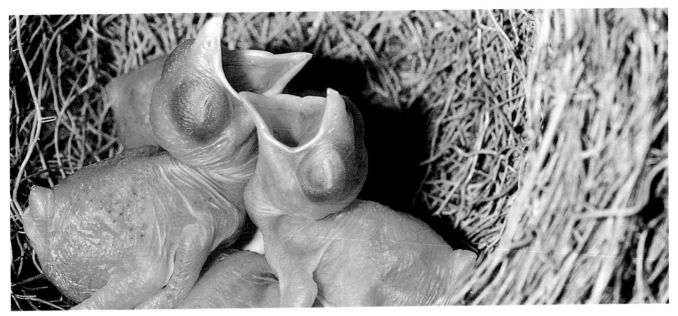

When songbirds hatch, they are featherless and blind. But, even at that stage, you can already see how big their eyes are going to be.

Some birds have eyes that are not just for seeing. The eyes of this demoiselle crane shine like rubies and help it to attract a mate.

COMPOUND EYES

The sight organs of insects can be made up of hundreds, or even thousands, of individual lenses and eyes. These organs are called "compound" eyes. Dragonflies, which can have over 20,000 lenses in each eye, may have the best sight of any insects.

Many flowers reflect light that our eyes cannot see. But a honeybee sees these colors in this light, which helps it find blossoms for making honey.

With its big compound eyes, this South American euglossine bee finds not only flowers, but also its colorful mate.

Wasps use their eyes to see quick movements, as well as colors, because they often hunt flying insects.

This rainforest grasshopper from South America has eyes designed especially for judging distances in the air so that it can jump and land safely.

Grasshoppers can see color—they have to recognize colors in order to find their food. They also use their good vision to avoid crashing while they are flying!

The common housefly can see objects moving about six times faster than human eyes are able to see. Flies can actually see the shape of a shooting bullet!

EIGHT-EYED CRAWLERS

Most spiders, including this jumping spider, have eight eyes. Since it searches for prey instead of waiting for it in a web, a hunting spider needs better vision than a web-spinning spider, which sees poorly.

Nothing gets by the jumping spider's eight eyes, which are distributed evenly around its head. The spider's large and powerful front eyes can spot unsuspecting prey far in the distance.

This hungry huntsman spider finds a hiding place and eagerly waits for an insect to happen by. The spider does not recognize its prey until the insect is close enough to be grasped.

This wolf spider has four large and four small eyes that give it a wide range of vision. Six of its eyes face forward while two point toward its sides.

A web-spinning spider has very poor vision. It must rely on its strong sense of touch to feel the movement of its prey, caught in its web.

SHARP, WATCHFUL EYES

Reptiles like this New Guinea gecko, rely heavily on their eyesight for survival. Although most reptiles' eyes work the same way on the inside, they can be quite different on the outside. Some reptiles' eyes have good night vision, while other reptiles' eyes are adapted for the day.

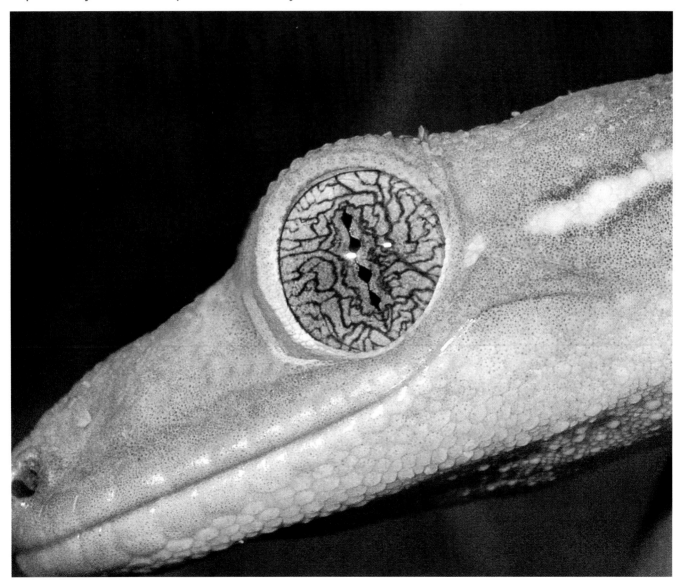

Like most geckos, this jungle gecko from Madagascar hunts insects at night. In the daytime, its pupils are thin slits. At night, however, they open into round circles.

Most geckos, like this web-footed gecko, cannot close their eyelids. They keep their vision clear by cleaning their eyes with their tongues!

A chameleon can move each eye independently. When it is hunting for insects, it can look up with its right eye and back with its left!

The eyes of a snake lack moveable eyelids, so snakes can't blink. The eyes of this longnosed tree snake, with their oddly shaped pupils, see particularly well at night.

This viper has a pit in front of each of its sharp eyes. The pit has a sense organ that feels the body heat of prey when it is near.

The slitty eyes of this dwarf puff adder look out from the desert sand, where the snake lies hidden, waiting for a mouse or lizard to come by.

This long, thin snake from Australia is called a brown tree snake. Its shining eyes are especially good for nighttime hunting.

FROGGY EYES

Though large eyes usually mean powerful vision, frogs don't see especially well. Most frogs, such as this tropical tree frog from Brazil, don't see a very clear picture. Instead, they notice movement and react very quickly.

The bright red eyes of the South American red-eyed tree frog are the only parts of its body that glow in the green rainforest.

Like its red-eyed relative, the yellow-eyed tree frog has eyes that seem to glow. Both frogs become active at night and have excellent night vision.

The round eyes of this tree frog from Peru sit high on its head, providing it with a good view in all directions.

The golden eyes of a toad see so poorly that a male will sometimes mistake a piece of wood for a female and hug it!

ANTENNA EYES

Humans aren't the only ones who think crabs make tasty meals. Crabs are vulnerable to many enemies, despite their hard shells. Most crabs, like this ghost crab, have good eyes that help them recognize danger quickly.

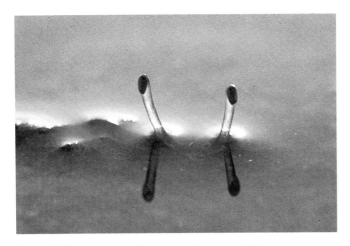

A crab's eyes sit on antenna-like stalks. This allows the crab to see what is happening outside a hiding place, or above water while it stays underwater.

Male fiddler crabs have one giant claw with a pattern that is different in each fiddler crab species, or group. These crabs use their claws and eyes to find a mate with a claw of the same pattern.

With its extremely powerful eyes, a ghost crab can spot a dangerous predator or unfortunate prey from a long distance in any direction.

Red-eyed crabs have very short eye stalks. Like all crabs, this one can pull its eyes down, with their stalks, into special pockets.

UNUSUAL EYES

Most animals have eyes with lenses, as we do. Some animals, such as insects, have compound eyes with many lenses. But there are other kinds of sight organs as well. Beneath their shells, these limpets (water snails) have cavities in their flesh with vision cells. The cells can only tell light from dark.

Some kinds of mollusks have simple eyes all along their fleshy sides, where their two shells meet. These eyes help mollusks, such as this giant clam, spot danger.

The dark point at each end of a slug's two antennae is an eye. A slug's eye can distinguish light and dark and can see movement.

Many animals that live in the dark—underground or at the bottom of the sea—have no eyes at all. One example is the termite shown here.

OPTICAL ILLUSIONS

Some animals have "eye spots" on their bodies that fool their enemies. The "false eyes" on the back of this caterpillar make it resemble a small, dangerous-looking snake, which may prevent predators from attacking.

This moth is hard to spot when it rests on a tree trunk because its color helps it camouflage itself, or blend in with its surroundings.

If the moth is discovered by a bird or another animal, it lifts its front wings and frightens its enemy with the two "eye spots" on its back wings.

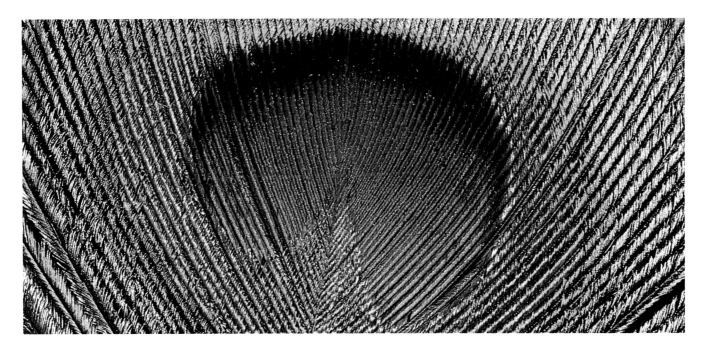

The beautiful eye-like markings on the tail feathers of a male peacock aren't there to frighten other animals. The male displays his "false eyes" to attract a female.

FOR FURTHER READING

Amstutz, Beverly. *The Fly Has Lots of Eyes.* Peachtree, GA: Precious Resources, 1981.

Greenway, Theresa. *Ears and Eyes.* Chatham, NJ: Raintree Steck-Vaughn Publishers, 1995.

Jedrosz, Aleksander. *Eyes.* Mahwah, NJ: Troll Communications, 1992.

Llamas, Andreu. *Sight.* New York: Chelsea House, 1996.

Savage, Stephen. *Eyes.* New York: Thomson Learning, 1995.

INDEX

Page numbers that include pictures are in italic.